100 More Ways to Keep Your Soul Alive

Frederic and Mary Ann Brussat

Praise for *100 Ways to Keep Your Soul Alive*

"This book of meditations does what it promises—helps keep (a wonderful word) soul present in daily life."
—THOMAS MOORE,
author of *Care of the Soul* and *Soul Mates*

"Simply the best take-out, gourmet soul-food available to delight and nourish the deep in you."
—SAM KEEN, author of *Fire in the Belly*

"There are only a finite number of great religious truths. Every religion has them all but often they are concealed. *100 Ways to Keep Your Soul Alive*, with creativity, power, and grace, spreads them all out before us. A great banquet."
—RABBI LAWRENCE KUSHNER,
author of *The Book of Words*

"Frederic and Mary Ann Brussat have provided us with an accessible treasure of the best that has been said about how to live life well."
—LEWIS B. SMEDES, author of *Shame and Grace*

"This book is a re-birthday cake with a hundred candles! Light one a day in your heart and share the gift."
—ALICE O. HOWELL, author of *The Web in the Sea*

"Reading this book is like walking along the ocean and finding one lovely stone after another. The difference is: with this book, you can actually use all the stones you find."

—JACOB NEEDLEMAN,
   author of *Money and the Meaning of Life*

100
More
Ways to
Keep Your
Soul Alive

100
More
Ways to
Keep Your
Soul Alive

Edited by
Frederic and Mary Ann Brussat

HarperSanFrancisco
A Division of HarperCollins*Publishers*

▧ A TREE CLAUSE BOOK

HarperSanFrancisco and the author, in association with
the Rainforest Action Network, will facilitate the planting
of two trees for every one tree used in the manufacture of
this book.

HarperCollins Web Site: http://www.harpercollins.com
HarperCollins®, ▉®, and HarperSanFrancisco™ are
trademarks of HarperCollins Publishers Inc.

Interior illustration by Kathleen Edwards
Book design by Martha Blegen

FIRST EDITION

Library of Congress Cataloging-in-Publication Data
100 more ways to keep your soul alive / edited by
Frederic and Mary Ann Brussat. —1st ed.
ISBN 0–06–251521–7 (pbk.)
1. Spiritual life—Quotations, maxims, etc. 2. Spiritual exercises. I. Brussat, Frederic. II. Brussat, Mary Ann.
BL624.A16 1997
291.4'3—dc21   97–2617

97 98 99 00 01 ❖ RRDH 10 9 8 7 6 5 4 3 2 1

To all the writers who have
nourished our souls

Contents

100 More Ways to Keep Your Soul Alive

Acknowledgments

We've been blessed to have a long career as book reviewers, a way of making a living that easily doubles as a way to keep our souls alive. For the opportunity to do this work, we are grateful to the members of our nonprofit organization, Cultural Information Service, to the subscribers to our various publications, and to those who have chosen to use material from the Values & Visions Reviews Service in their own publications and productions. We also thank the writers from whose books we have drawn inspiration and the quotations used here. To us, the world seems overflowing with wisdom!

Several people have been especially helpful as we have worked on this second volume of ways to live deeply and fully every day. Carolyn Dutton, our assistant, cleared the permissions for the book and also helped us clear the time to give it our attention. Our agent, Ned Leavitt, and his able associate, Kip Kotzen, took care of many important details.

We have thoroughly enjoyed working with our editor at HarperSanFrancisco, Caroline Pincus, from the first lunch when we met to talk about the sequel, through her thoughtful and enthusiastic response to the selection of quotes, to her immediate grasp of the importance of the practice suggestions, and her shepherding of the book through design and marketing. She's a pro we are pleased to have as a colleague. We also appreciate the help of others at HarperSanFrancisco, including editorial assistant Sally Kim, production editor Terri Leonard, copyeditor Kathy Reigstad, and designer Jim Warner. To Kathleen Edwards for her playful and soulful cover, bravo!

Finally, for all your expressions of support, spoken and unspoken, we are grateful to our families, friends, and the companions in our home.

Introduction

The idea for our first little book, *100 Ways to Keep Your Soul Alive*, came from a letter written by a character in a novel who was trying to care for her soul in challenging times. Our interest in doing a second collection also derives from correspondence—the many letters we received in response to that book.

We were a bit surprised by what readers said about *100 Ways to Keep Your Soul Alive*. It started as a collection of quotations from spiritual teachers, mystics, philosophers, activists, and artists. We felt that the passages chosen succinctly and beautifully identified the essential attitudes, perspectives, and actions that enable one to live deeply and fully—soulfully—every day.

What people commented upon most frequently in their letters and phone calls, however, weren't the quotations but the "first steps" that we added below them. These were suggestions of specific activities by which readers could try to put each "way" into "practice." Indeed, the importance of doing practices has been the lesson for us of that first book.

Here are some other things we've learned about keeping our souls alive as a spiritual practice:

- Practices of soulful living enable us to become actively engaged with our inner selves—the depth of our being—and with others around us—the breadth of our experiences in the world. Many also are seen as avenues to the Divine. All the world's religions encourage practice, but even without those endorsements, most people eventually discover that care of the soul requires some kind of intentional action.

- Practices are usually very concrete and practical. They specify just how we can walk our talk. Sometimes before we can act, however, we need to clarify our beliefs. Asking and living with questions is a kind of practice.

- A practice doesn't have to be hard. It rewards presence, not effort. Some practices do yield an outcome, but many are done simply for their own sake.

- Practice doesn't make perfect. To keep your soul alive, you don't need to become a master, overcome your weaknesses, or fix all your problems. As several passages in this book attest, difficulties are to be expected and can be used as aids on your journey.

- Practices bring out many of the activities associated with soulful living. They often lead to reflection, creativity, ritual, celebration, and play. Practice takes you to that sweet spot in time where spontaneity and passion both reside.
- Practice is process, and it changes over time. You may make a commitment to do a specific activity for years or you may get what you need from it in a day. The first steps in this book have that mixed quality of permanence and impermanence.
- Practices don't have to be complicated. Consider how many of the ritual exercises of the world's religions are simple: lighting a candle, eating a piece of bread, bowing. And don't disdain the use of your mind. Naming, remembering, watching, identifying, imagining—these are honored ingredients of the soulful life. The best practices for you will arise naturally out of your ordinary, everyday activities as you reframe and redirect them toward new depth and breadth.

The practice we use most often to keep our souls alive is reading. But, as this book and its predecessor testify, we also use reading as a catalyst for other forms of practice. The 100 ways mentioned in the title are both practices themselves and the inspiration for the more specific first steps that follow. The next time you're stirred by a moving passage of prose or poetry, try looking for the exercise hidden in the words.

One final point about practice: it leads to more practice. The ways presented in the pages ahead were all discovered in recent books, most of which are still available in libraries and bookstores. We hope that you'll browse through the Credits and Sources section at the back of the book and then look on your local shelves for those volumes that particularly interest you and for others by the same authors. There are favorite writers we return to again and again; but just as often it's by serendipity, and the conscious practice of hospitality, that we discover new voices who have the values and visions we need to keep our souls alive. May you adopt this practice as well.

I

Unwrap the Ordinary

Holiness comes wrapped in the ordinary. There are burning bushes all around you. Every tree is full of angels. Hidden beauty is waiting in every crumb. Life wants to lead you from crumbs to angels, but this can happen only if you are willing to unwrap the ordinary by staying with it long enough to harvest its treasure.

—Macrina Wiederkehr
in *A Tree Full of Angels*

Spend a weekend afternoon on a treasure hunt for the sacred in your experiences of the past week. Where did holiness shine through?

Look for Wisdom

Wisdom is hiding everywhere, but we haven't learned how to look, so that makes it very hard to see. It's a bit like those puzzles for children I remember, where you had to count how many animals you could find hidden in the picture of a tree. . . . It's certainly not the way most of us are educated to look.

—WALTER A. ANDERSEN
quoted in *The Dove in the Stone*

**Do a puzzle or play an optical illusion game.
What wisdom is revealed?**

3

Recognize Teachers

In the end, everyone is our teacher, on one level or another. The child is our teacher, our friends, our family, the stranger on the street. Every experience is a challenge; a teaching is always hidden in it. Every thought that bubbles up in our minds can teach us things about ourselves, if we are able to listen.

—DAVID A. COOPER
in Silence, Simplicity, and Solitude

**Name a person, thing, or activity
that has been a teacher to you.**

4

Read the World

The camel driver understood what the boy was saying. He knew that any given thing on the face of the earth could reveal the history of all things. One could open a book to any page, or look at a person's hand; one could turn a card, or watch the flight of birds . . . whatever the thing observed, one could find a connection with his experience of the moment. Actually, it wasn't that those things, in themselves, revealed anything at all; it was just that people, looking at what was occurring around them, could find a means of penetration to the Soul of the World.

—PAULO COELHO
in *The Alchemist*

Look around you.
Read the spiritual significance of something you see.

5

Discover Your Sacred Path

To walk a sacred path is to discover our inner sacred space: that core of feeling that is waiting to have life breathed back into it through symbols, archetypal forms like the labyrinth, rituals, stories and myths. Understanding the invisible world, the world of patterns and process, opens us up to the movement of the Spirit.

—LAUREN ARTRESS
in *Walking a Sacred Path*

**Describe the symbol or recount the story
that expresses your understanding of the invisible.**

6

Grow Spiritually

Growing spiritually can be like a roller coaster ride. Take comfort in the knowledge that the way down is only preparation for the way up.

—Rebbe Nachman of Breslov
in *The Empty Chair*

Draw a life map indicating the key turns, rises, and falls of your spiritual journey.

Watch for Diamonds

Life itself is hazardous.... There are sharp rocks everywhere. What changes from years of practice is coming to know something you didn't know before: that there are no sharp rocks—the road is covered with diamonds.

—CHARLOTTE JOKO BECK
in Nothing Special

**Reflect upon an event in your life
which at first seemed unpleasant but
turned out to be a blessing.**

8

Live Today

I heard a story about a man who went about the countryside asking people how they would spend their last day on earth. He came upon a woman who was out hoeing her garden, surrounded by her children and neighbor women. He decided he might as well ask her, too, even though he didn't expect much of an answer. "Woman," he asked, "if this were your last day on earth, if tomorrow it was certain you would die, what would you do today?"

"Oh," she said. "I would go on hoeing my garden and taking care of my children and talking to my neighbors."

—SUE MONK KIDD
in *The Dance of the Dissident Daughter*

**Regard what you are doing right now as a sacred task.
Don't allow yourself to be distracted.**

Sing Your Own Song

The woods would be very silent if no birds sang except the best.

—YIDDISH PROVERB
quoted in *Finding Joy*

Forget about what others are doing.
What is your special song?

Be Present

When Rikyu, Japan's legendary sixteenth-century tea master, was asked the secret of the Tea Ceremony, he replied, "Lighting the fire. Boiling the water. Whisking the tea." "Well, that seems easy to do," said the student. Rikyu responded, "If you can truly do this, then I will become your student."

—BETTINA VITELL
in *The World in a Bowl of Tea*

Be mindful when making your bed:
spreading the sheets, folding the corners,
smoothing the covers.

Welcome Spiritual Opportunities

Waiting for a bus, standing in line at the market or waiting to go into a bathroom during intermission at the theater becomes another chance to practice awareness. The usual frustrations of waiting and standing can be transformed into serious spiritual opportunity, a return to our pursuit of a more conscious, present existence grounded in respect for the sacred element in living.

> —DANIEL SINGER AND
> MARCELLA BAKUR WEINER
> in *The Sacred Portable Now*

**The next time you have to wait somewhere,
relax. Pay attention to your breath
and the input of your senses.**

Inspire Yourself

So many people don't know *how* to inspire themselves. Use everything that moves you: music, walking by water, flowers, photographs of the enlightened ones. Inspiration helps so deeply in overcoming laziness, summons what the Sufis call the fragrance of the Beloved into everything.

—ANDREW HARVEY
in *Dialogues with a Modern Mystic*

Compile a list of sources of inspiration for you, and set aside time to use one this week.

Become Beautiful

The purpose of the craft is not so much to make beautiful things as it is to become beautiful inside while you are making those things.

—SUSAN GORDON LYDON
in *The Knitting Sutra*

When you are engaged in your favorite hobby or craft, tap into the positive feelings you have about yourself.

Appreciate Music

Music can express the mystical experience better than language; it can tell of its mystery, joy, sadness, and peace far better than words can utter. The fatigued intellect finds a tonic and the harassed emotions find comfort in music.

—PAUL BRUNTON
   in *Meditations for People in Crisis*

Be attentive to any mystical feelings that surface when you are listening to music.

Simmer

I like food that is flavorful. Simmering food slowly, for a long time, helps the juices penetrate the whole. Hardly anyone simmers anything anymore. Everything is zapped in the microwave or cooked as quickly as possible. I think this reflects our spiritual life as well. Wisdom and wholeness deepen in us when we reflectively allow ideas and feelings to sit inside us for awhile.

—JOYCE RUPP
in *Dear Heart, Come Home*

Instead of responding immediately to a film, an art exhibit, a date, or a retreat, sit with the experience for a while before you process it.

Tune in to Your Body

When the body is finally listened to . . . it becomes eloquent. It's like changing a fiddle into a
Stradivarius. It gets much more highly attuned.

—MARION WOODMAN
in *Conscious Femininity*

**While walking, running, or swimming,
notice what your body is
communicating to you.**

Keep Your Body Healthy

Your body belongs to your ancestors, your parents, and future generations, and it also belongs to society and all other living beings. All of them have come together to bring about the presence of this body. Keeping your body healthy is an expression of gratitude to the whole cosmos—the trees, the clouds, everything.

—THICH NHAT HANH
in *Touching Peace*

Design a diet and exercise program that honors all those who contribute to your health and well-being.

Use Your Mind to the Hilt

Keep learning about the world.... Use your mind to the hilt. Life passes quickly and, toward the end, gathers speed like a freight train running downhill. The more you know, the more you enrich yourselves and others.

—SUSAN TROTT
in *The Holy Man*

**Start an independent learning project
or join a study circle. Explore a subject
you know little about.**

Write in a Journal

Keeping a journal thins my skin. I feel open to everything, aware . . . hypersensitive to whatever I hear, see, guess, read, am told. Matters that once might have gone unnoticed are no longer lost on me.

—DORIS GRUMBACH
in Extra Innings

Note your impressions of each day in a journal. After a week, see if you've kept something there that you might otherwise have lost.

Create a Place for Silence

When we make a place for silence, we make room for ourselves. This is simple. And it is radical. A room set apart for silence becomes a sanctuary—a place for breath, for refreshment, for challenge, and for healing. It is helpful to keep the space plain and simple: a few cushions, a rug . . . Simplicity allows the senses to rest from stimulation.

—GUNILLA NORRIS
in *Sharing Silence*

Decide what you need to do to transform a space in your home into a place for silence.

Step Aside

It is the creative person who steps aside from himself or herself and lets God through, who manifests otherworldly creations, celestial music, and spirit-filled stories. Even an ordinary person can accomplish extraordinary things when he or she steps aside and lets God in.

—SHONI LABOWITZ
in Miraculous Living

Act in a nonhabitual way.
For example, if you are right-handed,
write in your journal using your left hand.

Avoid Labeling

Labeling sets up an expectation of life that is often so compelling we can no longer see things as they really are. This expectation often gives us a false sense of familiarity toward something that is really new and unprecedented. We are in relationship with our expectations and not with life itself.

—RACHEL NAOMI REMEN
in *Kitchen Table Wisdom*

**For one day consciously give up
labeling everything. Monitor how this changes
the way you respond to new experiences.**

Practice Hospitality

Hospitality is not kindness. It is openness to the unknown, trust of what frightens us, the expenditure of self on the unfamiliar, the merging of unlikes. Hospitality binds the world together.

—JOAN CHITTISTER
in *In a High Spiritual Season*

Where do you meet the Other in your daily experience? How can you welcome it?

Kiss Monsters

Remember that sometimes monsters only need to be kissed to be turned into beautiful princes and princesses.

—MADELEINE L'ENGLE
in *Anytime Prayers*

Visualize the most despicable person you know.
Then envision the prince or princess
who also resides in him or her.

Plunge into Absurdity

One of the most powerful and effective ways of altering and undoing the routines of your life is to introduce some eccentricity, absurdity, and crazy wisdom. . . . Taking a plunge into its absurdity will trip you over yourself in a way that brings about powerful seeds for change while doing so with laughter and surprise rather than tears.

—BRADFORD KEENEY
in *Everyday Soul*

---

*What books, films, or TV situation comedies
are sources of crazy wisdom for you?*

Banish Separation

Separation is the arch-enemy of all life. Indeed the word "diabolical" is from the Greek *dia-ballein*, to separate or divide. So separation is the work of the devil, and let us away with it.

—ELAINE MACINNES
in *Light Sitting in Light*

Just say no to anyone who wants to split mind and body, head and heart, sacred and secular.

Get Some Perspective

Georgia O'Keeffe, the influential American painter, once suggested that everybody take a ride in an airplane. She thought the perspective from the airplane would change the way people see things. What is seen from airplane altitude is the connectedness of what appears from the ground level to be separated.

—JOHN SHEA
in *Starlight*

**Name situations when you are able
to grasp the big picture.**

Expand Your Vision of We

Dr. Beatrice Bruteau asks the right question: "How big is your *we*?" Can we expand our vision of community beyond our own skin, family, race, tribe, culture, country, and species? Spiritual life is more than what we believe, it also includes how we relate. Who is included in the *we* and who is not? That is both a spiritual and a political question. How we answer it will likely determine our future.

—Jim Wallis
in *Who Speaks for God?*

**Get to know someone from a different group
in your community.**

Open Up Your House

I do not want my house to be walled in on all sides and my windows to be shut. I want the cultures of all lands to be blown about my house as freely as possible.

—MAHATMA GANDHI
quoted in *Encountering God*

Walk through your home and count how many cultures are evident there.

Honor Your Companions

I have never forgotten the lesson a Buddhist once voiced. When you walk, be aware of those who walk alongside you, behind you, before you, of those on whose efforts you now stand. We are surrounded, says the writer of Hebrews, by a cloud of witnesses.

—JOAN PULS
in *Seek Treasures in Small Fields*

Say a prayer of appreciation to those invisible presences who accompany you on your spiritual journey.

Remember the Dead

As we grow older we have more and more people to remember, people who have died before us. It is very important to remember those who have loved us and those we have loved. Remembering them means letting their spirits inspire us in our daily lives.

—HENRI J. M. NOUWEN
in *Bread for the Journey*

Bring to mind loved ones who have died and the qualities you admired in them.

Image God

A little girl, drawing a picture, was asked by her mother: "What are you drawing?" She replied: "A picture of God!" "But we don't know what God looks like," her mother objected. "Well," replied the child, "when I am finished with this then you will know what God looks like!"

—RONALD ROLHEISER
in *Against an Infinite Horizon*

Make a drawing, painting, or collage of the image that best reflects your beliefs about God.

Hold Someone

The Society of Friends, known more widely as Quakers, have a practice called "holding someone in the Light." For the Friends, this is a kind of visual prayer, in which someone is held in God's love and illuminating presence.

—MARCY HEIDISH
in *Who Cares?*

Close your eyes and see someone who needs your support surrounded by the light of God.

Have a Moist Heart

Native Americans describe spirituality as having a "moist heart," perhaps because native wisdom knows the soil of the human heart is necessarily watered with tears, and that tears keep the ground soft. From such ground new life is born.

—MARIA HARRIS
in *Dance of the Spirit*

**Read a newspaper or magazine,
particularly the stories about pain
and suffering in the world.
Then have a good cry.**

Value Tiny Actions

It is said by the masters that even a little poison can cause death, and even a tiny seed can become a huge tree. And as Buddha said: "Do not overlook negative actions merely because they are small; however small a spark may be, it can burn down a haystack as big as a mountain." Similarly he said, "Do not overlook tiny good actions, thinking they are of no benefit; even tiny drops of water in the end will fill a huge vessel."

—SOGYAL RINPOCHE
in *The Tibetan Book of Living and Dying*

Review your actions during the past day.
Which were helpful?
Which were harmful?

Care About Things

Our alienation, our boredom, our estrangement can be cured only by the recovery of a philosophical sanity that will allow us to meet things face to face. An egg is an egg, and must be saluted as such. And china is china, and all things are themselves: mushrooms and artichokes, wine and cheese, earth and stars and sky and ocean. It is things that matter, and our cure waits for the restoration of our ability to care about them.

—Robert Farrar Capon
in *The Romance of the Word*

**Think of some ways to express your respect
for the things in your home or office.**

Save Treasures

When my wife was sixteen she played the lead role in her high school play, and someone gave her a bouquet of flowers. She kept one of the roses until it dried, and when the petals fell off, she put them in a box, which she has carried with her ever since. Now that the emotional connections to the play have faded, the object is important because it has been with her for so long.

—SHAUN MCNIFF
in *Earth Angels*

**Tell the story behind one object you've saved
or inherited from the past.**

Know What to Cut

Much of spiritual practice is just this: cutting away what must be cut, and letting remain what must remain. Knowing what to cut—this is wisdom. Being clear and strong enough to make the cut when it is time for things to go—this is courage. Together, the practices of wisdom and courage enable us, day by day and task by task, to gradually simplify our life.

—WAYNE MULLER
in *How, Then, Shall We Live?*

Commit to a process of simplifying your life by eliminating one excess behavior, project, or possession today.

Practice Generosity

Generosity has such power because it is characterized by the inner quality of letting go or relinquishing. Being able to let go, to give up, to renounce, to give generously—these capacities spring from the same source within us. When we practice generosity, we open to all of these liberating qualities simultaneously. They carry us to a profound knowing of freedom, and they also are the loving expression of that same state of freedom.

—SHARON SALZBERG
in *Lovingkindness*

Give away, without regrets, something you treasure.

Let Go

On the day of their marriage, Yvonne and her husband were given a rare and gorgeous antique Hopi vase. After the ceremony someone carried the vase on a tray with too many other things, and dropped it. The bowl broke into many pieces.

"A perfect moment," she smiled. "The bowl was only whole for the ceremony."

—SUE BENDER
in *Everyday Sacred*

Banish the word mine from your vocabulary.

Accept Imperfection

Native American cultures have a deep respect for the acceptance of our human imperfection. When weaving a rug, they will purposely include a flaw. This serves as a reminder that, while all that is humanly made is imperfect, it yet can reflect the beauty, reverence, care, and love of true creation.

—DIANE BERKE
in *The Gentle Smile*

Make peace with one of your imperfections.

See the Gracelets

We need to carve time for dwelling in the quiet places, to discover our own inner landscape and the landscape of God. We also must pay attention in the "cracks" of our life to see the "gracelets," the moments of meaning in the mundane.

—CELESTE SNOWBER SCHROEDER
in *Embodied Prayer*

Describe three incidents of grace you've witnessed.

43

Survey Your Wealth

Thurs. December 10, 1840: I discover a strange track in the snow, and learn that some migrating otter has made across from the river to the wood, by my yard and the smith's shop, in the silence of the night,—I cannot but smile at my own wealth, when I am thus reminded that every chink and cranny of nature is full to overflowing.—That each instant is crowded full of great events.

—HENRY DAVID THOREAU
quoted in *New and Selected Essays*

**Keep a notebook in which you describe
the signs and wonders you observe in
your immediate surroundings.**

Quit Whining

Maybe one day we'll grow weary of whining and celebrate the rain, the manna, the half-filled glass of water, the little gifts from heaven that make each day bearable. Instead of cloaking ourselves in the armor of pessimism, maybe we'll concede that we are who we are: capricious, unfortunate, wonderful, delicate, alive. Forgiven.

—MARK COLLINS
in *On the Road to Emmaus*

The next time you start complaining about your lot in life, don't listen.

45

Respect the Positive Voice

Don't make the "sophisticated" error of thinking that a negative voice is automatically smarter than a positive voice.

—MICHAEL VENTURA
in *Letters at 3 AM*

Cite an example of a sophisticated positive thought that has transformed your life.

Look on the Bright Side

Once there was a little tailor who was told his son had badly fractured his leg. The bearers of the news lamented, "Poor little tailor, to suffer such misfortune." But the tailor shrugged and replied, "Maybe not." The next day all the young men were drafted to fight in the czar's army except his son, exempted because of his leg.

—AVRAM DAVIS
in *The Way of Flame*

**No matter what happens to you today, say,
"This is good!"**

Don't Be Afraid of the Dark

In the midst of depression I once asked my spiritual director how I could be feeling such despair when not long before the depression hit I had been feeling so close to God? "Simple," she said. "The closer you get to light, the closer you get to darkness." The deepest things in life come not singly but in paradoxical pairs, where the light and the dark intermingle.

—PARKER PALMER
in *The Active Life*

Plan a ritual to celebrate inner and outer darkness.

Doubt

Doubting is not a sin. Nor does it denote a lack of faith. Lack of faith is a pure and simple disbelief. Doubting is an invitation to enter into the mystery more deeply, to go beyond the superficial.

JOHN AURELIO
in *Returnings*

Write a letter to your doubts, thanking them for the lessons they have taught you.

Love Paradox

We each possess a deeper level of being, . . .
which loves paradox. It knows that summer is
already growing like a seed in the depth of
winter. It knows that the moment we are born,
we begin to die. It knows that all of life shim-
mers, in shades of becoming—that shadow
and light are always together, the visible min-
gled with the invisible.

—GUNILLA NORRIS
in *Sharing Silence*

**Think about how paradox
has been evident in your journey.**

Raise Questions

To prevent questions from weighing us down, we must raise them. The longer we wait, the heavier they get, like a thatched roof in the rain. People who are afraid of raising questions run the risk of getting crushed under them. When we raise a question all the way, we find that the answer to every "Why?" is "Yes!" This sets us free.

—DAVID STEINDL-RAST
in *Gratefulness, the Heart of Prayer*

Identify the key question you are living with today.

Seek Guidance

Messenger signs can come on the waft of a candle's smoke, or in the gentle murmur of the wind, or in a dream, or from the thousand swirls of consciousness around you. These kinds of signs can give you direct messages from spirit. They can give you guidance about your spiritual development or a warning regarding future events. They can also give you a deeper understanding of the relationships and situations in your life.

—DENISE LINN
in *The Secret Language of Signs*

**Record one message you receive from Spirit today.
Be sure to credit the messenger.**

Have an Affair

Have the ultimate affair with the ultimate stranger: your shadow. Encounter the part of yourself you do not know. Have the ultimate affair—with your own soul. Find out about the parts of yourself that have been hidden from view.

—MARK GERZON
in *Listening to Midlife*

---

*Arrange a meeting between
your public self and your shadow.
What would they want to know about each other?*

Make Use of Your Vices

Do not give up your vices.
Make your vices work for you.

If you are a proud person,
don't get rid of your pride.
Apply it to your spiritual quest.

—JOSEPH CAMPBELL
in *Reflections on the Art of Living*

**Make a list of your vices.
Choose one and see how it can be an aid
to your spiritual practice.**

54

Acknowledge the Mystery of Good

The problem of evil has baffled mankind since Eden; perhaps because it can only be approached through facing the mystery of good, and we do not like to acknowledge that good is a mystery.

—D. M. DOOLING
in *Parabola*

**Remember a situation when you were amazed
by someone else's goodness to you,
a family member, or a friend.**

Be an Angel

I believe in angels, in our capacity to move with angels, bearing light and music, through this time and place.

Could you and I—like angels—learn to carry the good message? . . . Learn to be present when and where there is human need?

—TOBIAS PALMER
in *An Angel in My House*

Be an angel this day for your loved ones,
bearing messages of hope and renewal.

Join the Work of Planet-Saving

The real work of planet-saving will be small, humble, and humbling, and (insofar as it involves love) pleasing and rewarding. Its jobs will be too many to count, too many to report, too many to be publicly noticed or rewarded, too small to make anyone rich or famous.

—WENDELL BERRY
in Sex, Economy, Freedom, and Community

**Research volunteer opportunities with environmental
and service organizations in your community.
Select one to support with your time and money.**

Listen

Peoples of elder cultures often say that the sur-
vival of human beings depends on being able
to hear the language of the birds and beasts,
the language of the river, rock, and wind,
being able to understand what is being said in
all the tongues of plant, creature, and element.
Listening to the garbage as well as the rose
with the same ears, the ears of compassionate
understanding.

—JOAN HALIFAX
in *The Fruitful Darkness*

---

*Write down the messages you hear from your
garbage tonight—about where it comes from
and where it's going.*

Know Your Place

Whales and redwoods both make us feel small and I think that's an important experience for humans to have at the hands of nature. We need to recognize that we are not the stars of the show. We're just another pretty face, just one species among millions more.

—ROGER PAYNE
quoted in *Talking on the Water*

Visit the woods or the zoo.
Admire all the pretty faces there.

Cherish Gentleness

Gentleness values the softly spoken word, the tender touch, the warm embrace, and the kind, approving gesture. When we are in the presence of holy people, it is the power of their gentleness that moves us the most.... It is their consideration of others that brings forth their fullest presence.

—BRADFORD KEENEY
in *Everyday Soul*

Show gentleness in the way you treat an animal today.

Speak of Peace

When people talk about war
I vow with all beings
to raise my voice in the chorus
and speak of original peace.

—ROBERT AITKEN
in The Dragon Who Never Sleeps

**Express your opinion to your elected
representatives on a public policy issue
they are considering this month.**

Break the Silence

Listen. It's the silence of the small room after the torturers have left.

Listen. It's the silence in the councils of great nations when these difficult subjects are left unmentioned.

Listen. It's the silence of ordinary, decent people who think these things have nothing to do with them, and that they can do nothing to help.

Listen. Deep inside yourself. What do you hear? Break the silence.

> —AMNESTY INTERNATIONAL
> RADIO ADVERTISEMENT
> quoted in *The Tablet*

**Speak out against those who try
to stifle and extinguish the human spirit.
Support the work of human rights organizations.**

Forgive Others

A former inmate of a Nazi concentration camp was visiting a friend who had shared the ordeal with him.

"Have you forgiven the Nazis?" he asked his friend.

"Yes."

"Well, I haven't. I'm still consumed with hatred for them."

"In that case," said his friend gently, "they still have you in prison."

—ANTHONY DE MELLO
in *The Heart of the Enlightened*

**Share with a friend the healing that came to you
once you forgave someone and made
peace with the past.**

63

Forgive Yourself

Never forget that to forgive yourself is to release trapped energy that could be doing good work in the world. Thus, to judge and condemn yourself is a form of selfishness. Self-prosecution is never noble; it does no one a service.

—D. PATRICK MILLER
in *A Little Book of Forgiveness*

**Redirect the energy you've been using
to put yourself down into
a project to serve others.**

Be Easy in Your Heart

Be firm in your acts, but easy in your heart;
be strict with yourself, but gentle with your
fellowmen.

—CHINESE PROVERB
in *The World's Wisdom*

Use the phrase "be easy in your heart"
as a mantra today.
See how this practice colors your
interactions with others.

Express Your Feelings

The ability to feel is indivisible. Repress awareness of any one feeling and all feelings are
dulled. When we refuse to allow fear we corre-
spondingly lose the ability to wonder. When we
repress our grief we blunt our capacity to experience joy. The same nerve endings are required
for weeping and dancing, fear and ecstasy.

—SAM KEEN
in Fire in the Belly

**Find a creative way to express those feelings
that frighten you, the ones you keep hidden.**

Enjoy Travel

We were gone almost a month and everything was sensual. Everything was erotic. It's the gift of travel, where everything is infused with meaning, compressed, so you begin to see the golden strand that weaves life together. You are in a constant state of awe.

—TERRY TEMPEST WILLIAMS
quoted in *Listening to the Land*

**On your next trip, make an effort to commemorate
the most erotic, meaningful,
and awesome moments.**

Explore

I run into people all the time who are paralyzed by the fact that they might fail. To me, there's no failure. This is all an exploration.

—JOHN SAYLES
quoted in *Creating with the Angels*

**Evaluate your attitude toward failure.
Do you need to reframe it?**

Work with Muddy Water

The pure lotus growing in muddy water is a metaphor for enlightenment. The lotus arises from all its impediments. It actually needs the impurity of the water for its nourishment. In the same way, in our own personal development, we can't just work with what we like about ourselves. We have to work with our muddy water.

—BERNARD GLASSMAN
AND RICK FIELDS
in *Instructions to the Cook*

**Examine a personal problem or hang-up
and see how it can be a seedbed for new growth.**

Jump into the Void

If you jump into the void you could cease to exist, or you might emerge on the other side a new person. Precisely this gamble is at the heart of every redemption.

—LAWRENCE KUSHNER
in *The Book of Words*

Take a big risk.
Act without presuming to know
what will happen as a result.

Believe in the Resurrection

When you have the courage to marry
When you welcome the newly-born
    child
When you build your home
you believe in the resurrection.
When you wake at peace in the
    morning
When you sing to the rising sun
When you go to work with joy
you believe in the resurrection.

—CARLO CARRETTO
   in *Blessed Are You Who Believed*

**Consider how you are a life-bringer,
a resurrection person.**

Cultivate Zeal

There is no merit without zeal, just as there is no movement without wind. What is zeal? It is enthusiasm for virtue. What is said to be its antithesis? It is spiritual sloth, clinging to the reprehensible, apathy, and self-contempt.

—SANTIDEVA
in *A Guide to the Bodhisattva Way of Life*

**Review times during your life when
you've been zealous.
What sets you off?**

Do Small Things with Great Love

God has created us so we do small things with great love. I believe in that great love, that comes, or should come from our heart, should start at home: with my family, my neighbors across the street, those right next door. And this love should then reach everyone.

—MOTHER TERESA
in *Mother Teresa*

Invest the simple act of making breakfast with all the love you can muster. Imagine how this gesture has made the world a better place.

Keep Digging

Work. Keep digging your well.
Don't think about getting off from
    work.
Water is there somewhere.

Submit to a daily practice.
Your loyalty to that
is a ring on the door.

Keep knocking, and the joy inside
will eventually open a window
and look out to see who's there.

—Jelaluddin Rumi
    in *The Essential Rumi*

**Contemplate how your work can
bring you closer to Spirit.**

Don't Miss What's Happening

Radical openness is the invocation of full-bodied living, of first-hand experience. It is being unafraid to immerse ourselves in the full drama of being alive at this cusp in history, and to become participants in this great transitional moment as we move into the twenty-first century. It is not wanting to miss what's going on.

—VIVIENNE HULL
in *Earth and Spirit*

**Hurrah the most exciting aspects of life
at this point in history.**

Stop the World

Pleasure, like a glass of wine after hard work, stops the world, preparing an individual to be more receptive to the subtle nuances of his environment, luring him into reverie and reflection. . . . Pleasure is time-out.

—THOMAS MOORE
in *The Planets Within*

**Identify three things that give you pleasure.
Pause to enjoy one of them in
the middle of your day.**

Take a Break

My wife who is a religion teacher for primary grades tells me there is a time-honored tradition in her school, and it is this: Students from kindergarten and the first grade may with their teachers' encouragement go into another class and interrupt the lessons in progress. They do this for a very special purpose which they boldly announce through the use of a sign atop a stick which one of the group holds. The sign says: "*Poetry Break.*"

—ROBERT J. WICKS
in *After 50*

Read a favorite poem to a family member or friend.

Bring Others Stories

In some Islamic societies you would never bring a sick person flowers and candies as we do in this country. Instead, you would tell them a story of patience, endurance, and triumph. The images such a tale would plant in their awareness would circulate through their souls just as powerfully as a medicinal elixir would travel to the diseased cells by way of the bloodstream. The more the story is considered, the more it can empower the body's own healing mechanisms.

—RICHARD STONE
in *The Healing Art of Storytelling*

Collect healing stories from your life or the lives of others to tell during hospital visits.

Don't Ingest Toxins

We must also be careful to avoid ingesting toxins in the form of violent TV programs, video games, movies, magazines, and books. When we watch that kind of violence, we water our own negative seeds, or tendencies, and eventually we will think and act out of those seeds.

—THICH NHAT HANH
in *Living Buddha, Living Christ*

**Go on a violence fast.
Give up entertainments that contain
any kind of violence.**

Find Special People

Find those persons with whom you are comfortable. Find those persons in whose presence you feel more energetic, more creative and more able to pursue your life goals. Stay away from persons who make you feel apprehensive, or who influence you to doubt yourself. Especially, stay away from those persons who drain you, so that your energy is all used up in trying to maintain the relationship.

—DENNIS F. AUGUSTINE
in *Invisible Means of Support*

**Throw a party for the people in your life
who make it possible for you to be your best self.**

Practice Equanimity

There's one story about a monk who was begging and a woman who yelled at him, "You lazy monk, go do some work!" and poured a big bucket of water over his head. The monk got upset and angry. When he returned to the monastery, his teacher reminded him that in *takahatsu* everything, good or bad, should be accepted with equanimity. The monk, said the teacher, should have accepted the woman's anger as an offering.

—BERNARD GLASSMAN
AND RICK FIELDS
in *Instructions to the Cook*

This week don't let anything that happens outside of you determine whether you are grateful or mad, happy or sad.

Imitate the Valley

The valley accomplishes everything while doing nothing but being low and open.

By maintaining our modesty and by not considering anything beneath us, we can gain everything.

By being receptive, we can avail ourselves of the spiritual wealth available to us.

By being open, we can receive things beyond what we ourselves might imagine.

—DENG MING-DAO
in *Everyday Tao*

**Open your mind and heart to something
you've previously rejected.**

Don't Judge Others

In a world that constantly asks us to make up our minds about other people, a nonjudgmental presence seems nearly impossible. But it is one of the most beautiful fruits of a deep spiritual life and will be easily recognized by those who long for reconciliation.

—HENRI J. M. NOUWEN
in *Bread for the Journey*

**Restrain your tendency to evaluate
and criticize everyone you meet.**

Be a Mirror

Simply be the mirror in which others can see themselves as God sees them.

—EDWARD HAYS
in *The Gospel of Gabriel*

**Ask yourself: How do others see
themselves through me?**

Give

Initiate giving. Don't wait for someone to ask. See what happens—especially to you. You may find that you gain a greater clarity about yourself and about your relationships, as well as more energy rather than less.

—JON KABAT-ZINN
in *Wherever You Go, There You Are*

Surprise someone with an unexpected gift.

Cultivate Resiliency

Blades of grass
Bent silently beneath the shoe,
Springing back—silently.

—KENNETH VERITY
in Breathing with the Mind

**Create a ritual in which you act out
the quality of resiliency.**

Do What You Are Supposed to Do

Everyone in this life has something they are supposed to do. If you don't do what you are supposed to do, you have terrible bad luck.

—ROLLING THUNDER
quoted in *The Wizdom Within*

**Write a description of a job that would use
most of your gifts and skills.**

Embrace Tedium

A person works in a stable.
That person has a breakthrough.
What does he do?
He returns to work in the stable.

—MEISTER ECKHART
in *Meditations with Meister Eckhart*

**Apply one of your spiritual insights to
the most menial task you do.**

Stay Put

Since Einstein, we have learned that there is no center; or alternatively, that any point is as good as any other for observing the world. . . . There are no privileged locations. If you stay put, your place may become a holy center, not because it gives you special access to the divine, but because in your stillness you hear what might be heard anywhere. All there is to see can be seen from anywhere in the universe, if you know how to look; and the influence of the entire universe converges on every spot.

—SCOTT RUSSELL SANDERS
in *Staying Put*

**Sit quietly in your living room or backyard.
Contemplate how you are connected to the universe.**

Be a Sanctuary

My whole life, in one sense, has been an experiment in how to be a portable sanctuary—learning to practice the presence of God in the midst of the stresses and strains of contemporary life.

—RICHARD J. FOSTER
in *Prayers from the Heart*

Come up with two new ways to take your prayers and praise into the world.

Remain at Home

I was passionate,
filled with longing,
I searched
far and wide.

But the day
that the Truthful One
found me,
I was at home.

—LAL DED
in *Women in Praise of the Sacred*

**Through dance or embodied prayer, express your
thanks to Spirit for being present in your home.**

Put Out to Sea

Pilgrim
When your ship
long moored in harbour
gives you the illusion
of being a house;
when your ship begins to
put down roots
in the stagnant water
by the quay
PUT OUT TO SEA!

Save your boat's journeying soul
and your own pilgrim soul
cost what it may.

—HELDER CAMARA
quoted in *The Archetype of Pilgrimage*

**Start an activity that will expand your horizons and
take you to places you have never been.**

Be Grateful

We think that people are grateful because they are happy. But is this true? Look closely, and you will find that people are happy because they are grateful. When we are thankful for whatever is given to us, no matter how difficult, no matter how uninvited it may be, the thankfulness itself makes us happy.

—DAVID STEINDL-RAST
in *The Music of Silence*

**Identify what stops you from being grateful
for everything that comes your way.**

Do Something Silly

Finding true joy is the hardest of all spiritual tasks. If the only way to make yourself happy is by doing something silly, do it.

—REBBE NACHMAN OF BRESLOV
in *The Empty Chair*

Fashion a "Feast of Fools" holiday when you and your loved ones do silly and outrageous things just for the joy of it.

Utter Blessings

Blessings keep our awareness of life's holy potential ever present. They awaken us to our own lives. . . . With each blessing uttered, we extend the boundaries of the sacred and ritualize our love of life.

—LAWRENCE KUSHNER
in *The Book of Words*

Compose blessing prayers for some of the people, animals, plants, buildings, and objects you encounter today.

Want What You Have

Rabban Gamliel used to say:

Desire only that which has already been given.
Want only that which you already have.

—RABBAN GAMLIEL
quoted in *Wisdom of the Jewish Sages*

Do the hardest thing of all: ask for nothing else.

Check on Your Heart

Many native cultures believe that the heart is the bridge between Father Sky and Mother Earth. For these traditions, the *four-chambered heart*, the source for sustaining emotional and spiritual health, is described as being full, open, clear, and strong. These traditions feel that it is important to check the condition of the four-chambered heart daily, asking: "Am I full-hearted, open-hearted, clear-hearted, and strong-hearted?"

—ANGELES ARRIEN
in *The Four-Fold Way*

Assess the health of the four chambers of your heart. Which need attention?

Observe How Worlds Touch

I was driving along in a companionable silence with a niece of mine when she was about six. She turned to me suddenly with a beatific smile on her face and announced cryptically that words were wonderful things because they contained information about many worlds and how the different worlds touch. When pressed for an explanation, she said that a tree had to do with the world of the sky—the sun, rain and wind. It also had to do with the earth and the worms. Everything was connected. Little Alexa had stumbled upon the concept of inter-dependence.

—JOAN BORYSENKO
in *A Woman's Book of Life*

Recall an incident when you vividly sensed the interconnectedness of life. What happened?

Change

This is how a human being can change:

there's a worm addicted to eating
grape leaves.
　　Suddenly, he wakes up,
call it grace, whatever, something
wakes him, and he's no longer
a worm.
　　He's the entire vineyard,
and the orchard too, the fruit, the trunks,
a growing wisdom and joy
that doesn't need
to devour.

　　　　　—JELALUDDIN RUMI
　　　　　　in *The Essential Rumi*

**Celebrate a moment when you saw the world
with fresh eyes.**

Dance with God

God is the lead dancer and the soul is the partner completely attuned to the rhythm and patterns set by the partner. She does not lead, but neither does she hang limp like a sack of potatoes.

> —THOMAS MERTON
>   quoted in *Listening to the Music
>   of the Spirit*

**See yourself dancing with God.
What images and feelings come to you?**

Win More Than You Lose

Life is not a trap set for us by God, so that He can condemn us for failing. Life is not a spelling bee, where no matter how many words you have gotten right, if you make one mistake you are disqualified. Life is more like a baseball season, where even the best team loses one-third of its games and even the worst team has its days of brilliance. Our goal is not to go all year without ever losing a game. Our goal is to win more than we lose, and if we can do that consistently enough, then when the end comes, we will have won it all.

—HAROLD S. KUSHNER
in *How Good Do We Have to Be?*

**Imagine the scoreboard of your life.
Count everything as a win.**

Credits and Sources

Grateful acknowledgment is made for permission to reprint the following material:

1. Quotation from page xiii of *A Tree Full of Angels* by Macrina Wiederkehr. Copyright © 1988 by Macrina Wiederkehr. Reprinted by permission of HarperCollins Publishers, Inc.

2. Walter A. Andersen quoted in *The Dove in the Stone* by Alice O. Howell. Wheaton, IL: Quest Books, 1988. Used by permission of Quest Books.

3. From *Silence, Simplicity and Solitude* by David Hanoch Cooper. Copyright © 1992 by David Hanoch Cooper. Reprinted by permission of Bell Tower, an imprint of Harmony Books, a division of Crown Publishers, Inc.

4. Quotation from page 106 of *The Alchemist* by Paulo Coelho. Translated by Alan R. Clarke. Copyright © 1988 by Paulo Coelho. English translation copyright © 1993 by Paulo Coelho and Alan R. Clarke. Reprinted by permission of HarperCollins Publishers, Inc.

5. Reprinted by permission of Riverhead Books, a division of the Putnam Publishing Group, from *Walking a Sacred Path* by Lauren Artress. Copyright © 1995 by Lauren Artress.

6. From *The Empty Chair: Finding Hope and Joy—Timeless Wisdom from a Hasidic Master, Rebbe Nachman of Breslov*. Copyright © by The Breslov Research Institute. Permission granted by Jewish Lights Publishing, Sunset Farm Offices, Rte. 4, P.O. Box 237, Woodstock, VT 05091.

7. Quotation from page 114 of *Nothing Special: Living Zen* by Charlotte Joko Beck and Steven A. Smith. Copyright © 1993 by Charlotte Joko Beck. Reprinted by permission of Harper-Collins Publishers, Inc.

8. Quotation from *The Dance of the Dissident Daughter* by Sue Monk Kidd. Copyright © 1996 by Sue Monk Kidd. Reprinted by permission of HarperCollins Publishers, Inc.

9. Yiddish proverb quoted in *Finding Joy* by Dannel I. Schwartz. Woodstock, VT: Jewish Lights Publishing, 1997.

10. Quotation from page 3 of *The World in a Bowl of Tea* by Bettina Vitell. Copyright © 1997 by Bettina Vitell. Reprinted by permission of HarperCollins Publishers, Inc.

11. From the book *Sacred Portable Now.* Copyright © 1997 by Daniel Singer and Marcella Bakur Weiner. Rocklin, CA: Prima Publishing, 800–632–8676.

12. Andrew Harvey in *Dialogues with a Modern Mystic.* Wheaton, IL: Quest Books, 1994. Used by permission of Quest Books.

13. Quotation from page 137 of *The Knitting Sutra: Craft as a Spiritual Practice* by Susan Gordon Lydon. Copyright © 1997 by Susan Gordon Lydon. Reprinted by permission of HarperCollins Publishers, Inc.

14. Reprinted with permission of Larson Publications from *Meditations for People in Crisis* by Paul Brunton, edited by Sam and Leslie Cohen. Burdett, NY.

15. Joyce Rupp in *Dear Heart, Come Home.* New York: Crossroad Publishing Co., 1996. Used by permission of Crossroad Publishing Co.

16. Marion Woodman in *Conscious Femininity* from *Studies in Jungian Psychology by Jungian Analysts, No. 58.* Daryl Sharp, general editor. Toronto: Inner City Books, 1993. Used by permission of Daryl Sharp.

17. Reprinted from *Touching Peace: The Art of Mindful Living* (1992) by Thich Nhat Hanh, with permission of Parallax Press, Berkeley, CA.

18. Reprinted by permission of Riverhead Books, a division of the Putnam Publishing Group, from *The Holy Man* by Susan Trott. Copyright © 1995 by Susan Trott.

19. From *Extra Innings* by Doris Grumbach. Copyright © 1993 by Doris Grumbach. Reprinted by permission of W.W. Norton & Company, Inc., and Russell & Volkening, Inc.

20. From *Sharing Silence: Meditation Practice and Mindful Living* by Gunilla Norris. Copyright © 1993 by Gunilla Norris. Reprinted by permission of Bell Tower, an imprint of Harmony Books, a division of Crown Publishers, Inc.

21. Reprinted by permission of Simon & Schuster from *Miraculous Living* by Rabbi Shoni Labowitz. Copyright © 1996 by Rabbi Shoni Labowitz.

22. Reprinted by permission of Riverhead Books, a division of the Putnam Publishing Group, from *Kitchen Table Wisdom* by Rachel Naomi Remen, M.D. Copyright © 1996 by Rachel Naomi Remen.

23. Joan Chittister in *In a High Spiritual Season*. Liguori, MO: Triumph Books, 1995. Used by permission of Triumph Books.

24. Reprinted from *Anytime Prayers* by Madeleine L'Engle. Copyright © 1994 by Madeleine L'Engle. Used by permission of Harold Shaw Publishers, Wheaton, IL 60189.

25. Reprinted by permission of Riverhead Books, a division of the Putnam Publishing Group, from *Everyday Soul* by Bradford Keeney, Ph.D. Copyright © 1996 by Bradford Keeney.

26. Quotation from pages 14–15 of *Light Sitting in Light* by Elaine MacInnes. Copyright © 1996 by Elaine MacInnes. London: HarperCollins/Fount.

27. John Shea in *Starlight*. New York: Crossroad Publishing Co., 1992. Used by permission of Crossroad Publishing Co.

28. From *Who Speaks for God?* by Jim Wallis. Copyright © 1996 by Jim Wallis. Used by permission of Delacorte, a division of Bantam Doubleday Dell Publishing Group, Inc.

29. Mahatma Gandhi quoted in *Encountering God* by Diana Eck. Boston: Beacon Press, 1993.

30. Joan Puls in *Seek Treasures in Small Fields*. Mystic, CT: Twenty-Third Publications, 1993. Used by permission of the author.

31. Selection dated August 29 from *Bread for the Journey* by Henri J. M. Nouwen. Copyright © 1996 by Henri J. M. Nouwen. Reprinted by permission of HarperCollins Publishers, Inc., NY, and Darton, Longman and Todd Ltd., London.

32. Ronald Rolheiser in *Against an Infinite Horizon*. New York: Crossroad Publishing Co., 1995. Used by permission of Crossroad Publishing Co.

33. Marcy Heidish in *Who Cares?* Notre Dame, IN: Ave Maria Press, 1997. Used by permission of the author.

34. From *Dance of the Spirit* by Maria Harris. Copyright © 1989 by Maria Harris. Used by permission of Bantam Books, a division of Bantam Doubleday Dell Publishing Group, Inc.

35. Quotation from page 92 of *The Tibetan Book of Living and Dying* by Sogyal Rinpoche. Copyright © 1993 by Rigpa Fellowship. Reprinted by permission of HarperCollins Publishers, Inc.

36. Robert Farrar Capon in *The Romance of the Word*. Grand Rapids, MI: Wm. B. Eerdmans Publishing, 1995. Used by permission of Wm. B. Eerdmans Publishing.

37. From *Earth Angels* by Shaun McNiff. Copyright © 1995 by Shaun McNiff. Reprinted by arrangement with Shambhala Publications, Inc., 300 Massachusetts Avenue, Boston, MA 02115.

38. From *How, Then, Shall We Live?* by Wayne Muller. Copyright © 1996 by Wayne Muller. Used by permission of Bantam Books, a division of Bantam Doubleday Dell Publishing Group, Inc.

39. From *Lovingkindness* by Sharon Salzberg. Copyright © 1995. Reprinted by arrangement with Shambhala Publications, Inc., 300 Massachusetts Avenue, Boston, MA 02115.

40. Quotation from page 92 of *Everyday Sacred* by Sue Bender. Copyright © 1995 by Sue Bender. Reprinted by permission of HarperCollins Publishers, Inc.

41. Diane Berke in *The Gentle Smile*. New York: Crossroad Publishing Co., 1995. Used by permission of Crossroad Publishing Co.

42. Celeste Snowber Schroeder in *Embodied Prayer*. Liguori, MO: Triumph Books, 1994. Used by permission of Triumph Books.

43. Henry David Thoreau quoted in *New & Selected Essays* by Denise Levertov. New York: New Directions, 1992.

44. Mark Collins in *On the Road to Emmaus*. Liguori, MO: Liguori Publications, 1994. Used by permission of Liguori Publications.

45. Michael Ventura in *Letters at 3 AM*. Dallas, TX: Spring Publications, 1993. Used by permission of Spring Publications.

---

46. Quotation from page 93 of *The Way of Flame* by Avram Davis, Ph.D. Copyright © 1996 by Avram Davis, Ph.D. Reprinted by permission of HarperCollins Publishers, Inc.

47. Quotation from page 102 of *The Active Life* by Parker Palmer. Copyright © 1990 by Parker Palmer. Reprinted by permission of HarperCollins Publishers, Inc.

48. From *Returnings: Life-After-Death Experiences: A Christian View* by John Aurelio. Copyright © 1995. Reprinted by permission of the Continuum Publishing Company, NY.

49. From *Sharing Silence: Meditation Practice and Mindful Living* by Gunilla Norris. Copyright © 1993 by Gunilla Norris. Reprinted by permission of Bell Tower, an imprint of Harmony Books, a division of Crown Publishers, Inc.

50. Quoted from *Gratefulness, the Heart of Prayer* by Brother David Steindl-Rast. Copyright © 1984 by David Steindl-Rast. Used by permission of Paulist Press.

51. Denise Linn in *The Secret Language of Signs*. New York: Ballantine Books, 1996. Used by permission of Ballantine Books, an imprint of Random House.

52. From *Listening to Midlife* by Mark Gerzon. Copyright © 1996. Reprinted by arrangement with Shambhala Publications, Inc., 300 Massachusetts Avenue, Boston, MA 02118.

53. Quotation from page 135 of *Reflections on the Art of Living: A Joseph Campbell Companion*, selected and edited by Diane Osbon. Copyright © 1991 by the Joseph Campbell Foundation. Reprinted by permission of HarperCollins Publishers, Inc.

54. "Fire Proveth Iron" by D. M. Dooling. Reprinted from *Parabola, the Magazine of Myth and Tradition*, Vol. 10, No. 4 (Winter 1985). Used by permission of *Parabola*.

55. Quotation from *An Angel in My House* by Tobias Palmer. Copyright © 1994 by Winston Weathers. Reprinted by permission of HarperCollins Publishers, Inc.

56. Wendell Berry in *Sex, Economy, Freedom and Community*. Copyright © 1993 by Wendell Berry. Used by permission of Pantheon Books, a division of Random House, Inc.

57. Joan Halifax in *The Fruitful Darkness*. Copyright © 1993 by Joan Halifax. San Francisco: HarperSanFrancisco, 1993. Reprinted by permission of the author.

58. "Voices from the Sea" by Roger Payne, from *Talking on the Water*, edited by Jonathan White. Copyright © 1994 by Jonathan White. Reprinted with permission of Sierra Club Books.

59. Reprinted by permission of Riverhead Books, a division of the Putnam Publishing Group, from *Everyday Soul* by Bradford Keeney, Ph.D. Copyright © 1996 by Bradford Keeney.

60. Reprinted from *The Dragon Who Never Sleeps* (1992) by Robert Aitken, with permission of Parallax Press, Berkeley, CA.

61. Amnesty International banned radio advertisement. Reprinted with permission of *The Tablet*, the international Catholic weekly, July 1, 1995.

62. From *The Heart of the Enlightened* by Anthony de Mello. Copyright © 1989 by The Center for Spiritual Exchange. Used by permission of Doubleday, a division of Bantam Doubleday Dell Publishing Group, Inc.

63. D. Patrick Miller in *A Little Book of Forgiveness*. Copyright © 1994 by D. Patrick Miller. Published by Viking Penguin, a division of Penguin Books USA Inc.

64. Chinese proverb from *The World's Wisdom: Sacred Texts of the World's Religions* by Philip Novak. Copyright © 1994 by Philip Novak. Reprinted by permission of HarperCollins Publishers, Inc.

65. From *Fire in the Belly* by Sam Keen. Copyright © 1991 by Sam Keen. Used by permission of Bantam Books, a division of Bantam Doubleday Dell Publishing Group, Inc.

66. Quote by Terry Tempest Williams from *Listening to the Land* by Derrick Jensen. Copyright © 1995 by Derrick Jensen. Reprinted with permission of Sierra Club Books.

67. John Sayles quoted in *Creating with the Angels* by Terry Lynn Taylor. Tiburon, CA: H.J. Kramer, 1993.

68. From *Instructions to the Cook* by Bernard Glassman and Rick Fields. Copyright © 1996 by The Zen Community of New York and Rick Fields. Reprinted by permission of Bell Tower,

an imprint of Harmony Books, a division of Crown Publishers, Inc.

69. From *The Book of Words: Talking Spiritual Life, Living Spiritual Talk*, by Lawrence Kushner. Copyright © by Lawrence Kushner. Permission granted by Jewish Lights Publishing, Sunset Farm Offices, Rte. 4, P.O. Box 237, Woodstock, VT 05091.

70. Carlo Carretto in *Blessed Are You Who Believed*. Maryknoll, NY: Orbis Books, 1983. Used by permission of Orbis Books, Maryknoll, NY, and Burns & Oates, Kent, England.

71. Santideva in *A Guide to the Bodhisattva Way of Life*, translated by Vesna A. Wallace and B. Alan Wallace. Ithaca, NY: Snow Lion Publications, 1997.

72. Mother Teresa in *Mother Teresa: In My Own Words* by Jose Luis Gonzalez-Balado. Liguori, MO: Liguori Publications, 1996. Used by permission of Liguori Publications.

73. Jelaluddin Rumi in *The Essential Rumi*, translated by Coleman Barks with John Moyne, A. J. Arberry, and Reynold Nicholson. HarperSanFrancisco, 1995. Reprinted by permission of Coleman Barks.

74. From *Earth & Spirit: The Spiritual Dimension of the Environmental Crisis*, edited by Fritz Hull. Copyright © 1993. Reprinted by permission of the Continuum Publishing Company, NY.

75. Thomas Moore in *The Planets Within*. Hudson, NY: Lindisfarne Books, 1990. Used by permission of Lindisfarne Books.

76. Quoted from *After 50: Spiritually Embracing Your Own Wisdom Years* by Robert J. Wicks. Copyright © 1997 by Robert J. Wicks. Used by permission of Paulist Press.

77. Richard Stone in *The Healing Art of Storytelling*. New York: Hyperion, 1996. Used by permission of Hyperion.

78. Reprinted by permission of Riverhead Books, a division of the Putnam Publishing Group, from *Living Buddha, Living Christ* by Thich Nhat Hanh. Copyright © 1995 by Thich Nhat Hanh.

79. From *Invisible Means of Support: A Transformational Journey* by Dr. Dennis F. Augustine. Copyright © 1994 by Dennis F. Augustine. Used by permission of Golden Gate Publishing.

80. From *Instructions to the Cook* by Bernard Glassman and Rick Fields. Copyright © 1996 by The Zen Community of New York and Rick Fields. Reprinted by permission of Bell Tower, an imprint of Harmony Books, a division of Crown Publishers, Inc.

81. Quotation from page 253 of *Everyday Tao* by Deng Ming-Dao. Copyright © 1996 by Deng Ming-Dao. Reprinted by permission of HarperCollins Publishers, Inc.

82. Selection dated December 27 from *Bread for the Journey* by Henri J. M. Nouwen. Copyright © 1996 by Henri J. M. Nouwen. Reprinted by permission of HarperCollins Publishers, Inc., NY, and Darton, Longman and Todd Ltd., London.

83. Edward Hays in *The Gospel of Gabriel*. Copyright © 1996 by Edward Hays. Reprinted with permission of Forest of Peace Publishing, Inc., 25 Muncie Road, Leavenworth, KS 66048.

84. Jon Kabat-Zinn in *Wherever You Go, There You Are*. Copyright © 1994 by Jon Kabat-Zinn. New York: Hyperion. Used by permission.

85. Kenneth Verity in *Breathing with the Mind*. Copyright © 1993 by Kenneth Verity. Used by permission of Element Books.

86. Rolling Thunder quoted in *The Wizdom Within* by Susan Jean and Dr. Irving Oyle. Tiburon, CA: H.J. Kramer Inc., 1992.

87. Meister Eckhart in *Meditations with Meister Eckhart* by Matthew Fox. Santa Fe, NM: Bear & Company, 1983. Used by permission of Bear & Company.

88. Scott Russell Sanders in *Staying Put*. Boston: Beacon Press, 1993.

89. Quotation from page xi of *Prayers from the Heart* by Richard J. Foster. Copyright © 1994 by Richard J. Foster. Reprinted by permission of HarperCollins Publishers, Inc.

90. Poem by Lal Ded, translated by Jane Hirshfield, from *Women in Praise of the Sacred: 43 Centuries of Spiritual Poetry by Women*. Jane Hirshfield, editor. Copyright © 1994 by Jane Hirshfield. Reprinted by permission of HarperCollins Publishers, Inc., and Jane Hirshfield.

91. Archbishop Helder Camara quoted in *The Archetype of Pilgrimage* by Jean Dalby Clift and Wallace B. Clift. Mahwah, NJ: Paulist Press, 1996.

92. Quotation from pages 36–37 of *The Music of Silence* by Brother David Steindl-Rast and Sharon Lebell. Copyright © 1995 by Brother David Steindl-Rast and Sharon Lebell. Reprinted by permission of HarperCollins Publishers, Inc.

93. From *The Empty Chair: Finding Hope and Joy—Timeless Wisdom from a Hasidic Master, Rebbe Nachman of Breslov.* Copyright © by The Breslov Research Institute. Permission granted by Jewish Lights Publishing, Sunset Farm Offices, Rte. 4, P.O. Box 237, Woodstock, VT 05091.

94. From *The Book of Words: Talking Spiritual Life, Living Spiritual Talk* by Lawrence Kushner. Copyright © by Lawrence Kushner. Permission granted by Jewish Lights Publishing, Sunset Farm Offices, Rte. 4, P.O. Box 237, Woodstock, VT 05091.

95. Rabban Gamliel quoted in *Wisdom of the Jewish Sages* by Rami Shapiro. Copyright © 1993 by Rami M. Shapiro. Reprinted by permission of Bell Tower, an imprint of Harmony Books, a division of Crown Publishers, Inc.

96. Quotation from page 50 of *The Four-Fold Way* by Angeles Arrien. Copyright © 1993 by Angeles Arrien. Reprinted by permission of HarperCollins Publishers, Inc.

97. Reprinted by permission of Riverhead Books, a division of the Putnam Publishing Group, from *A Woman's Book of Life* by Joan Borysenko, Ph.D. Copyright © 1996 by Joan Borysenko.

98. Jelaluddin Rumi in *The Essential Rumi*, translated by Coleman Barks with John Moyne, A. J. Arberry, and Reynold Nicholson. HarperSanFrancisco, 1995. Reprinted by permission of Coleman Barks.

99. Thomas Merton quoted in *Listening to the Music of the Spirit* by David Lonsdale. Notre Dame, IN: Ave Maria Press, 1993.

100. From *How Good Do We Have to Be?* by Harold S. Kushner. Copyright © 1996 by Harold S. Kushner. Originally published by Little, Brown and Company. Reprinted by permission of Curtis Brown, Ltd.

About the Editors

Frederic and Mary Ann Brussat have been covering contemporary culture and the spiritual renaissance for thirty years through their work with Cultural Information Service and their publications, including *Values & Visions* magazine. The Values & Visions Reviews Service provides book, movie, video, and audio reviews to magazines, newspapers, radio stations, the Odyssey cable TV network, and the Ecunet computer network.

The Brussats are the directors of the Values & Visions Circles, an international network of small discussion groups who use movies, videos, books, and spoken-word audios as catalysts to soul-making. They have created more than 250 *Values & Visions Guides* for these groups and for interested individuals.

The Brussats' first book, *100 Ways to Keep Your Soul Alive*, was published by HarperSanFrancisco in 1994. *Spiritual Literacy: Reading the Sacred in Everyday Life* was published by Scribner in 1996.

Frederic is a United Church of Christ clergyman with a journalism ministry. The Brussats live in New York City.

For more information on the Brussats' work, write:

CIS/Values & Visions Circles
P.O. Box 786, Dept. 100M
Madison Square Station
New York, NY 10159
USA